# Dream Boat

For Mom and Dad,
for Halina,
and in memory of Winifred Owen

# Contents

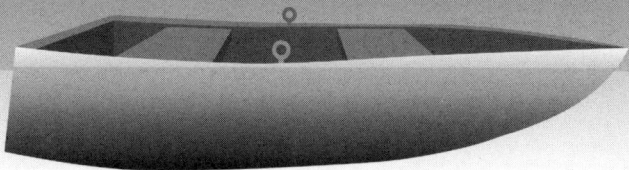

# Chapter 1

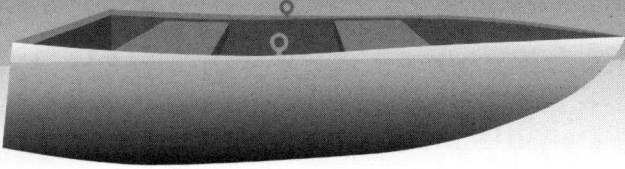

It was *finally* summer! Jessie had been looking forward to it since her birthday last month. Mom and Dad had said she was now old enough to take out their rowboat by herself.

As she rushed home from her last day of school, she couldn't help stopping in front of the next-door neighbor's fence. Jessie really liked mysteries, and she was sure that there was something *strange* going on behind that tall fence.

I'm sure that the boat can wait a few more minutes, she told herself.

With Jessie, mysteries always came first, and she wanted to get to the bottom of what her neighbor Mr. Silas was hiding behind his fence.

She crouched down on one knee and looked through a tiny hole in the fence. She saw grass and part of the house as well. Something was different this time, but she wasn't sure what it was.

Suddenly, Jessie felt as if someone was watching her. She turned and found herself face to face with Mr. Silas. He was carrying a screwdriver and a hammer, and he was staring at Jessie suspiciously.

"I thought I heard something out here," he said. "I've told you before to stay off my property."

"I wasn't doing..." Jessie began, but she couldn't think of what to say next.

Mr. Silas looked as if he was about to start yelling. Jessie knew it was impossible to talk sense with Mr. Silas.

So, instead, she dodged around him and ran toward her house.

When she turned around, she saw Mr. Silas squinting through the hole in the fence.

# Chapter 2

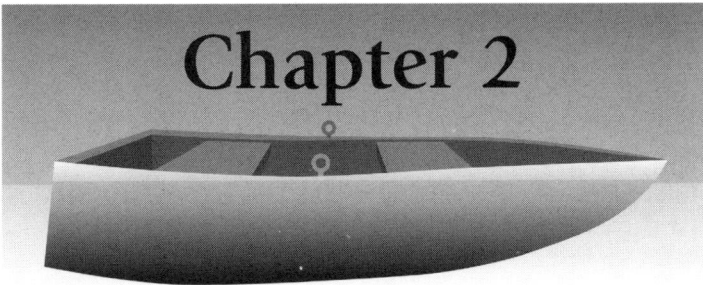

"Here we go," Dad said when Jessie arrived home, eager to finally take out the boat. "Let's get you out on the water."

The rowboat was kept upside down on the lawn under the plum tree, close to the water. Ducks sometimes sat on the keel. It was too heavy for Jessie to turn over without help.

So together, Jessie and her dad righted the boat. They pushed it down the bank until it bobbed in the creek, still tied to the plum tree.

"Do you need a hand getting in?"

"I can handle it, Dad," Jessie said, lowering herself into the boat. They'd named it *Silver Birch,* after the silver birch trees that lined the creek.

She fit the oars into the oarlocks.

"Don't forget your life jacket," Mom reminded her.

"I know," Jessie said, putting it on.

"It's too bad we don't have any champagne," Dad said.

"Why?" Jessie asked.

"To launch the boat. To celebrate the solo voyage of Jessie Hayes on board the good ship *Silver Birch.*"

"Hold on," Mom said. "I have an idea." She ran to the house and returned with a plastic bottle. "How about soda pop?" she said, shaking it.

"It's going to fizz up and explode," Jessie warned.

"That's the idea," Mom said, unscrewing the top. The soda pop shot out over the boat. Some of it splashed on Jessie.

"That is a really weird custom, Mom," Jessie laughed, wiping off her face.

"Weird or not, it's anchors aweigh," Dad said, untying the rope.

Jessie rowed the boat into the center of the creek. "I'm not going far now. This is just practice for tomorrow," she called over her shoulder.

First, she rowed downstream with the current, then upstream against it. It felt great. Half an hour later she rowed up to the bank. She tossed out the rope, climbed out, and tied the boat to the plum tree.

Once the boat was secured, Jessie got back into it to think about her plan.

She decided to see if she could use the rowboat to get to Mr. Silas's back gate. With a little luck, she could open the gate and find out what he was hiding.

# Chapter 3

That night, Jessie couldn't get to sleep. Her plan filled her head. And, for some reason, she kept hearing strange noises. Finally, she got up.

"What's going on?" she asked.

Sounds of banging and wrenching were coming from next door.

"It sounds like the end of the world," Dad said. "I'll take a look and try to see what that old guy is up to."

While he was gone, Jessie remembered the hammer and screwdriver that Mr. Silas had been carrying that afternoon when she'd come home from school.

He must be patching that hole she'd been looking through.

She had a terrible thought – if he was being that careful about his privacy, it probably meant he'd be sure to have his back gate locked, too.

"Is Mr. Silas working on his fence?" she asked when her dad returned.

"Well, I suppose you could say that," Dad said. "Actually, he's tearing out the whole front fence."

"Why?" Jessie and Mom exclaimed together.

"That's anybody's guess. I wasn't about to ask. I'll tell you one thing, though. That house of his is a real eyesore. It would have been better if he'd kept it hidden."

"So what's wrong with his house?" Jessie asked.

Dad counted off all the bad things. "One, a lot of the wood looks rotten. Two, most of the paint has flaked off. Three, the whole yard is a wilderness. Four, he has a black sheep grazing on his front lawn."

"A real live sheep?" Jessie asked. Maybe it was a guard sheep. She'd just have to get past it...

"Now, Jessie," said Dad, "you keep away from that animal. It's not tied up, and it looks as tough as an old iron bar."

"You mean an old iron ba-aa-a!" Jessie giggled as she imitated the bleating of a sheep and headed back to bed.

That night, she dreamed of a wild, wooly black sheep named Iron Baa, who was in charge of guarding a secret, hidden treasure.

# Chapter 4

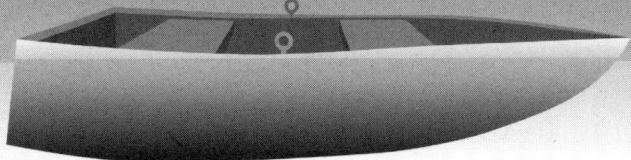

The next morning, Jessie was up very early. She wanted to get over to Mr. Silas's place before he was up. After all, she thought, he must be pretty tired after working so late last night.

She made herself some granola and chopped apple. Mom and Dad were still asleep. She decided to make them some breakfast, too, so they wouldn't be too cross when she woke them up to say she was going. She balanced the tray as she tapped at their door.

"Jessie?" Mom said, rubbing her eyes. "What time is it?"

"It's early," Jessie whispered. "I'm taking the boat out, remember?"

"Oh yes. Be careful. How far are you going today?"

"Only as far as Mr. Silas's house."

"Watch out for old 'Iron Baa,'" Dad said. "That sheep will probably be pretty cranky after all that noise last night."

"What time did Mr. Silas finish?" Jessie asked.

"He worked until well past midnight," Dad said. Before he could continue, the house suddenly started to tremble.

Dad jumped out of bed, and he and Jessie ran to the window.

"It's a huge truck!" Jessie said.

Dad opened the window and leaned out as far as he could. "I can't see where it went, but I bet it's over at Mr. Silas's place."

"I'm already dressed," Jessie said. "I'll see what's going on and report back."

"Don't let him catch you snooping. You know how mad it makes him," Dad called after her.

Jessie ran up the road. Mr. Silas was standing in his yard, calling instructions to the driver, who was backing the rig up to the house.

When Jessie saw the house, her mouth dropped open in astonishment. The house was about three feet up off the ground and was sitting on large, square blocks. No wonder it had looked different yesterday when she'd squinted at it through the hole in the fence.

Then Jessie saw Iron Baa for the first time. It was big and black and wooly. It looked just like the guard sheep in her dream, but it didn't seem fierce.

Iron Baa raced away from the trailer and escaped to the safety of the backyard.

That's when Mr. Silas spotted Jessie. "Scram!" he shouted. "Stop pestering me. I don't want sightseers."

Rats! He'd spotted her. Jessie turned back toward home.

"Guess what!" she said to Mom and Dad as she walked in. "I think Mr. Silas's house is being taken away."

After she'd told them what she'd seen, she went out to the rowboat, thinking. Other than the house looking so strange, she hadn't seen anything that seemed mysterious. But Mr. Silas was still trying to keep her away. That must mean he was still hiding something, and that something must be in his backyard.

# Chapter 5

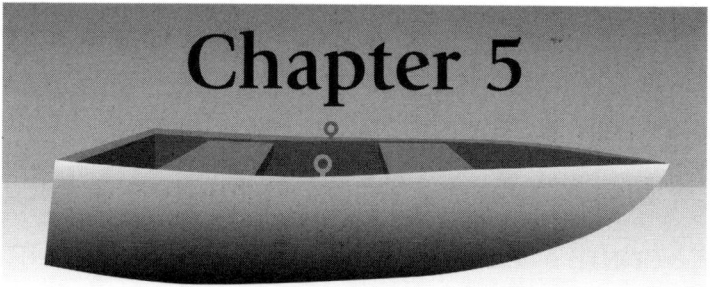

The splash of oars in the water disturbed the stillness of the early morning as Jessie set out.

For the second time that morning, she arrived at Mr. Silas's, but this time she was at the back of his yard, and this time she hoped she'd stay unseen.

Jessie rowed the boat to the bank and tied it to a tree. As she took off her life jacket, her heart was beating faster than it had while she was rowing. She went to Mr. Silas's back gate and pushed on it. A small part of her hoped it would be locked.

But the gate swung open, and Jessie peeked inside.

She really hadn't planned to go any farther. What she saw, however, made her step through the gate. Mr. Silas did have a secret, and it was worth discovering.

Inside the fence, there was a boat.

It wasn't a small boat like *Silver Birch*. It was huge. It was so large, it made the rest of the yard look tiny. But because of where it was placed, the old house had completely hidden it from anyone who might have looked in from the street.

The black sheep, who Jessie couldn't help but think of as Iron Baa, watched her as she walked around the boat, touching the bright paint. The boat's name was painted in curling red letters on the white bow. The letters were big, but the words didn't make any sense.

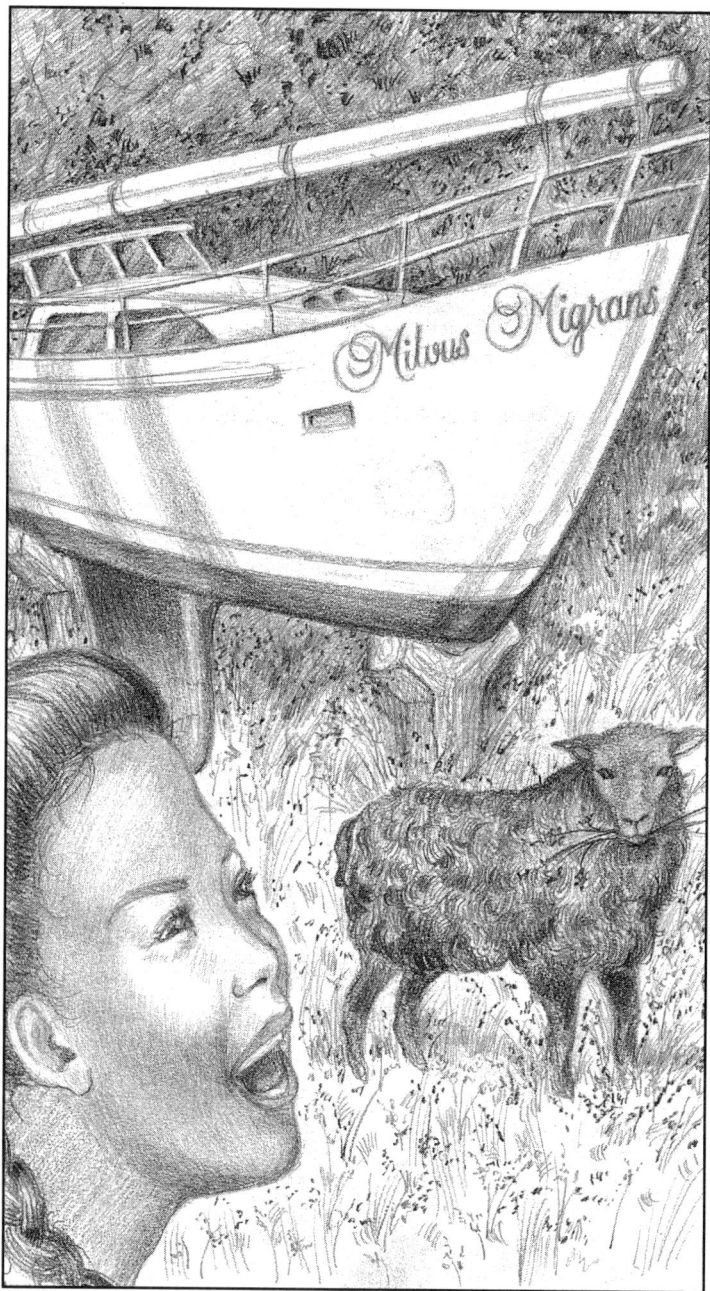

The boat's name reads "Milvus Migrans"

Jessie tried saying the name aloud, "*Milvus Migrans.*"

It still didn't make any sense.

On her second walk around the boat, Jessie bumped into Mr. Silas.

"Whoops!" she gulped. She had forgotten all about him in the excitement of finding the boat.

Mr. Silas glared at her. "You again! Didn't I tell you to stay away from here?"

Jessie could only nod.

"Then what are you doing?"

"Investigating," Jessie said in a small, frightened voice.

"Trespassing is what I'd call it. How'd you get in here?"

Jessie took a deep breath. "The back gate was open," she said in a rush. "I wasn't going to come inside, honest. But I saw the boat and I couldn't help it."

Mr. Silas walked to the back gate. He noticed *Silver Birch.*

"Is that yours?" he asked, sounding a little less angry.

"It's ours. My parents' and mine. We live next door to you."

Mr. Silas looked Jessie in the eye. "Do you like boats?"

"I like mysteries best," she said, "but I like boats, too. Yours is beautiful."

"I call it my dream boat," he said, as if he had decided to share a secret with her. "I built it myself. It took me twenty years, but it's been worth every minute." He looked off into the distance.

"People said I'd never finish it," he added. "They thought I was crazy. They couldn't see anything happening, so it became a joke. They said it was just my crazy dream. But I knew I'd finish it."

"Is that why you hid it?" Jessie asked, her confidence returning.

"Would you want your dream to be someone else's joke?" Mr. Silas asked in return. "Anyway, I no longer care what other people think of me or of my dream. I did it to make myself happy. You're the only other person who knows about it."

"But when the house gets taken away..." Jessie began.

Mr. Silas laughed for the first time. "Let's try to keep it a secret," he said. "Tonight I'll be gone."

"Where to?"

"Everywhere," said Mr. Silas. "*M.M.*'s an oceangoing sailboat, and no ocean will be too big for it. Now you'll have to go away. I have some last-minute details to take care of."

"What about the sheep?" Jessie asked, pointing toward Iron Baa as Mr. Silas hurried her out.

"She'd get seasick," Mr. Silas said. "And she prefers grass to salt water. You can have her when I've left."

And then he shut the gate on Jessie, hiding his dream once more behind the tall fence.

# Chapter 6

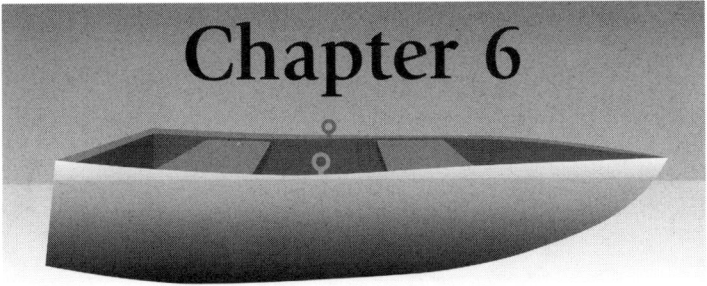

Jessie tied up *Silver Birch* and went racing into the house. "Mom! Dad! Guess what!"

"What's up, Jessie?" Dad asked.

"Mr. Silas has an oceangoing sailboat behind his house!" Jessie said breathlessly. "He said that people used to laugh at him about it, so he hid it behind the fence. He's been building that boat for years and years and years. It's called..."

She shut her eyes, trying to remember. "*Milvus Migrans*," she said slowly. "What does that mean?"

"I don't know," Mom said, "but we can find out."

"An oceangoing sailboat? Are you sure he doesn't just have a small pleasure boat, Jessie?" Dad asked.

"No," Jessie insisted. "Dad, you're the one who taught me the difference. In fact, you'll be able to see it when the house is moved."

In the afternoon, Mom went to the library to return some books. When she returned, she looked pleased with herself. "I found out what *Milvus Migrans* means," she said.

"What?" Jessie asked eagerly.

"I looked it up in a Latin dictionary. *Milvus* is a kite, but not the kind you fly. A kite is also a kind of bird. *Migrans* means migrating. You know, traveling from one place to another."

"The traveling bird," Jessie said. "That's a good name for a boat."

"I thought so, too," Mom said.

It was dark when the truck finally left with Mr. Silas's house perched on it. Things had started happening much later than Jessie had hoped.

"We have to see what's going on over there," she begged.

But Dad was firmly against it, and Mom agreed with him.

"We'll go over first thing tomorrow, when it's light enough to see something," Dad said. "Mr. Silas wouldn't take his boat anywhere tonight."

"But he said…"

"Tomorrow, Jessie," Dad said.

Mr. Silas was waiting on purpose, Jessie thought. This way, no one would see him leave. But *I* will.

# Chapter 7

Jessie was determined to see the boat go. She believed that Mr. Silas had meant it when he'd said he was leaving that night. She did everything she could to stay awake. She read by flashlight. She played word games. She played with her stuffed animals.

When Mom and Dad finally went to bed, Jessie got up. She put on her robe and slippers and crept quietly into the warm night.

Before long, a truck pulling an empty trailer drove down the street. It disappeared into Mr. Silas's yard.

"This is it," Jessie whispered. But she had to wait nearly a half hour before the truck reappeared, pulling *Milvus Migrans* on its trailer.

Jessie felt sad. Mr. Silas really was leaving, and he was taking his dream away with him. If it had been Jessie's boat, she knew she never could have sneaked away like this. She would have told the whole street the boat was finally finished – and shown everybody that she had made her dream come true.

As it was towed from the yard, the beautiful dream boat looked like a bird about to launch itself in flight.

Mr. Silas saw her. His mouth opened in surprise. He and Jessie managed a brief wave to each other. Moments later the truck, Mr. Silas, and *Milvus Migrans* were gone.

# Chapter 8

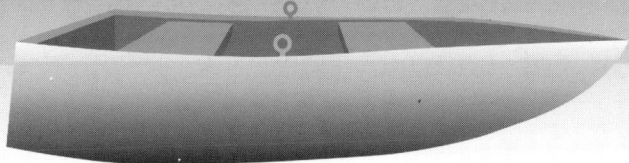

Jessie slept late the next morning. This time she dreamed about a boat that was flying over the waves.

"Jessie! Come on, sleepyhead. Get up!" Dad said, gently shaking her awake.

"Dad. The boat! I saw it go."

"You were dreaming. I already went to take a look. Believe me, Jessie, there's no boat, sailboat or otherwise. No Mr. Silas either. There was just that weird sheep glaring at me."

So Mr. Silas had been serious about leaving the sheep, too. Iron Baa was her responsibility now.

Jessie suddenly felt angry at Dad and betrayed by Mr. Silas. Dad was right, of course. There wasn't a boat there anymore. How would anyone ever know that there had been one?

"I want to go and see for myself."

"OK," Dad said, "if you insist."

Mom came, too. They walked to where Mr. Silas's house had been. A few other neighbors had also come to stare at the empty lot.

"He left without a word," one neighbor said. "He was a strange guy."

"He left his sheep behind, though," a lady chuckled.

"Keep away from it," Dad said to Jessie, who was trying to approach the sheep. "It'll bite you or something."

"Mr. Silas said I could have her," Jessie answered.

"We can't keep a sheep!" Dad said.

"But she just eats grass," Jessie pleaded as Iron Baa nuzzled into her stomach. "See? I'm all she has now."

Then Jessie found the note tied around Iron Baa's wooly neck.

"What is it?" Mom asked.

"It's a letter from Mr. Silas!"

Her parents read over her shoulder.

Dear Girl,

I'm on my way to Africa. If you don't know why, look in a book about birds. I'm happy you saw my boat yesterday. You can go ahead and tell everyone my dream came true.

Sincerely,

Mr. Silas

P.S. I never gave my sheep a name, so you choose one.

"Who'd have believed it?" Dad said.

"Africa," Mom said. "He's going a long way." She sounded envious. Even Dad had a faraway look in his eyes.

"Why do I have to look in a book about birds?" Jessie asked.

"*Milvus migrans* is an African bird," Mom explained.

Jessie nodded. She still felt sad, but the sadness was mixed with a kind of happiness. Mr. Silas was traveling on the bird he had made – his dream boat. And no one would doubt it anymore.

"Come on, Iron Baa," she said. "Let's go back to our place."

Jessie led Iron Baa to the sheep's new home. And to Jessie, Iron Baa was now a reminder to her to make all her dreams come true.

# Dreams

*Hold fast to dreams*

*For if dreams die*

*Life is a broken-winged bird*

*That cannot fly.*


**– Langston Hughes**

## From the Author

I live in Christchurch, New Zealand, where I work as a librarian. My stories have been published in magazines and anthologies, and have been broadcast on television and radio as well. One of my inspirations for *Dream Boat* came from seeing a large boat hidden behind a fence and wondering how it was ever going to reach the sea.

**Bill Nagelkerke**

## From the Illustrator

I love illustrating children's books. Because of my involvement with the theater, I am always struck by how much illustrating a book is like putting on a play. I cast the parts, pick the costumes and props, then play out each scene with my pencils and paintbrushes.

I like the message I discovered in *Dream Boat:* Follow your dreams even when others laugh at you.

### Connie Marshall

"Dreams" from *Collected Poems* by Langston Hughes. Copyright © 1994 by the Estate of Langston Hughes. Reprinted by permission of Alfred A. Knopf, Inc.

This book was completed with the help of a grant from the Literature Program of the Queen Elizabeth II Arts Council of New Zealand, to which grateful acknowledgement is made.

Written by **Bill Nagelkerke**
Illustrated by **Connie Marshall**
Edited by **Rebecca McEwen**
Designed by **Pat Madorin**
Author photograph by **H.T. Keenan**. Copyright © 1997.

02 01 00 99 98 97
10 9 8 7 6 5 4 3 2 1

Distributed in the United States by
**Rigby**
a division of Reed Elsevier Inc.
P.O. Box 797
Crystal Lake, IL 60039-0797

Printed by Colorcraft, Hong Kong
ISBN: 1-57257-732-0